ANIMALS GROWING UP™

HOW EAGLES GROW UP

Heather Moore Niver

E **Enslow Publishing**
101 W. 23rd Street
Suite 240
New York, NY 10011
USA

enslow.com

WORDS TO KNOW

aerie A large nest that is built high in the air, especially an eagle's nest.

brood A family, especially of birds, including the young.

carnivore An animal that eats meat.

clutch A group of eggs laid at about the same time.

down Fluffy fuzz covering baby birds.

eaglet A baby eagle.

fledging Growing the feathers needed to fly, or learning to fly.

mate To come together to have babies.

species A group of the same kind of living thing that have the same scientific name.

CONTENTS

FLYING HIGH

More than 60 species, or kinds, of eagles are found all over the world. In North America, there are bald eagles and golden eagles. Golden eagles live in Europe, Asia, and Africa, too.

FAST FACT

Bald eagles were named because from far away, their white feathers make their heads look bald.

A golden eagle's head is brown (*left*). A bald eagle's head is white (*right*).

NEST SWEET NEST

Bald eagles spend about 20 weeks building their aeries, or nests, and raising their young. During this time, they stay close to home. Eagles lay eggs in the same nest for several years.

A bald eagle and her babies sit in their nest on the side of a cliff.

FAST FACT

Eagles may return to the same nest several years in a row. They add to it each year, making it bigger and stronger.

EAGLE EGGS

Most eagles lay one to three eggs at a time. A group of eggs is called a **clutch**. Both parents sit on the nest to keep them warm and safe.

FAST FACT

Eagles mate for life. This means two eagles will stay together to raise babies.

Two eagle eggs lie in a nest.

EAGLETS HATCH

Both golden and bald eagle babies, called eaglets, take more than a month to hatch. Then it is about another two months before they will try flying.

FAST FACT

Golden and bald eaglets are born with gray down. Then they grow gray feathers.

These eaglets are covered in soft fuzz called down.

GROWTH SPURTS

Eaglets grow quickly! Bald eagles can gain one pound (half a kilogram) every four or five days. After two weeks, they are strong enough to hold up their heads to be fed.

FAST FACT

Adult eagles curl their sharp talons into a ball to keep from hurting their eaglets in the nest.

Bald eaglets wait for their parents to bring them food.

PROTECTING CHICKS

The mother protects her brood, or family. Eaglets are born helpless. While they are in the nest, they are called nestlings. Bald eagles start to leave the nest after about 70 days.

Eagles learn to fly by walking out of the nest.

A bald eagle guards her nestlings.

HUNGRY BABIES

Eaglets grow so fast, they are very hungry! Their parents spend almost all their time hunting for food to feed their hungry babies. Both parents help hunt for and feed them.

A bald eagle brings food to the nestlings.

FAST FACT

Eagles are **carnivores**. They eat fish, small mammals, other birds, and reptiles.

LEARNING TO FLY

Eagles remain in the nest for several weeks. But soon they have the feathers they need to fly. This is called **fledging**.

FAST FACT

Golden eaglets may fly between 65 and 70 days after they hatch, while bald eagles wait 78 to 82 days.

A bald eagle fledgling stretches its wings.

FEATHERS

Bald eagles' heads and tails turn white around four or five years of age. Golden eagles grow brown feathers with gold on their heads and necks.

A golden eagle has golden brown feathers as an adult.

FAST FACT

Bald eagles live to be about 35 years old or even older in the wild. Golden eagles may live to 38 years.

EDUCATING EAGLES

When they are older, bald eaglets learn from the adults. They hang out and watch the older eagles catch fish. Eaglets also try to steal food from their parents!

Bald eagles leave the nest at 17 to 23 weeks of age.

A bald eagle catches a fish. Soon, her eaglets will learn to feed themselves and be on their own.

23

LEARN MORE

Books

Jennings, Rosemary. *Eagles.* New York, NY: PowerKids Press, 2016.

Kissock, Heather. *Bald Eagles.* New York, NY: AV2 by Weigl, 2017.

Renne. *The Eagle: Animals in the Wild.* New York, NY: Clavis Publishing, 2017.

Websites

National Geographic Kids: Bald Eagle
kids.nationalgeographic.com/animals/bald-eagle/#bald-eagle-closeup.jpg
Check out more fun facts about bald eagles.

San Diego Zoo Kids: Golden Eagle Tonka
kids.sandiegozoo.org/videos/golden-eagle-tonka
Watch a video about a golden eagle named Tonka and learn more facts about how golden eagles live and act.

INDEX

Published in 2019 by Enslow Publishing, LLC.
101 W. 23rd Street, Suite 240, New York, NY 10011

Copyright © 2019 by Enslow Publishing, LLC.
All rights reserved.

No part of this book may be reproduced by any means without the written permission of the publisher.

Library of Congress Cataloging-in-Publication Data

Names: Niver, Heather Moore, author.
Title: How eagles grow up / Heather Moore Niver.
Description: New York, NY : Enslow Publishing, 2019. | Series: Animals growing up | Includes bibliographical references and index. | Audience: Grades K to 3.
Identifiers: LCCN 2017044745| ISBN 9780766096394 (library bound) | ISBN 9780766096400 (pbk.) | ISBN 9780766096417 (6 pack)
Subjects: LCSH: Eagles—Infancy—Juvenile literature.
Classification: LCC QL696.F32 N58 2017 | DDC 598.9/42—dc23
LC record available at https://lccn.loc.gov/2017044745

Printed in the United States of America

To Our Readers: We have done our best to make sure all website addresses in this book were active and appropriate when we went to press. However, the author and the publisher have no control over and assume no liability for the material available on those websites or on any websites they may link to. Any comments or suggestions can be sent by email to customerservice@enslow.com.

Photo Credits: Cover, p. 1 Takayuki Maekawa/The Image Bank/Getty Images; pp. 4–23 (background image), 19 Jennifer Bosvert/Shutterstock.com; p. 5 (left) Jesus Giraldo Gutierrez/Shutterstock.com; p. 5 (right) Dr. Alan Lipkin/Shutterstock.com; p. 7 Paul Reeves Photography/Shutterstock.com; p. 9 Lori Skelton/Shutterstock.com; p. 11 Alexander Prosvirov/Shutterstock.com; p. 13 Brian Guzzetti/First Light/Getty Images; p. 15 Ron Niebrugge/Alamy Stock Photo; p. 17 BirdImages/E+/Getty Images; p. 21 Michal Ninger/Shutterstock.com; p. 23 Brian E Kushner/Shutterstock.com.